CRYPTO CURRENCIES INSIGHTS

PISHU SHAMDASANI

To order additional copies of this book, contact
Toll Free +65 3165 7531 (Singapore)
Toll Free +60 3 3099 4412 (Malaysia)
www.partridgepublishing.com/singapore
orders.singapore@partridgepublishing.com

ISBN
978-1-5437-7165-7 (sc)
978-1-5437-7167-1 (hc)
978-1-5437-7166-4 (e)

Print information available on the last page.

09/30/2022

PARTRIDGE

Contents

Aum.......

CRYPTO CURRENCIES INSIGHTS

Life dynamics have changed faster than jet speed through emerged and yet emerging technologies. Each one of us regardless of ethnicity, gender or age are being affected in many profound ways. While it is not necessary to know how technology works, if we know and learn what technology does, then at the very least we can get by with present day life. i.e. WhatsApp, email and several other simple yet very useful functions.

Presently the norm is online shopping, online banking, online ordering of groceries and food, online dispersal of money by governments through digital systems and such others. Even travel to many places has adopted use of e-tickets, online check-ins, self-check-ins, mobile and other online payments digitally, replacing tedious, time-consuming analogue systems as used in the recent past.

Technologies are now being commonly used in several aspects of life and will continue being used much more faster going forward in time. It is thus imperative that we learn and adapt to those technologies which apply to our personal day to day life, Banking, Finance, Investments, savings, withdrawals, deposits. and the like. Our young children are very nimble and many of us in our late 50's, 60's request our children to help us with digital matters i.e. filling online application forms, banking, etc. It is understandable that we cannot approach others or unknown persons for reasons of safety and security.

To serve the above purpose the author of this e-book has undertaken to share the insights of some of the important technologies that are now being deployed essentially in several aspects of everyday life.

> "Adventurous heroism, Daring courage
> Faith in self, Consistency of purpose
> Intellectual heroism"
> -Shrimad Geeta

WHAT ARE CRYPTO CURRENCIES?

They are digital currencies, enabled by wondrous immutable blockchain technology in which transactions are verified and accurate, irreplaceable, and irreversible. The transactions cannot be destroyed or adjusted in any way by any individual, a group, or a corporate body. Records are kept utilizing cryptography instead of centralized authorities i.e. governments or banks and even note issuing banks or reserve banks.

Decentralized crypto currencies i.e. Bitcoin, Ethereum, Solana, Polkadot and thousands of others now provide an outlet for personal wealth that is beyond restriction and confiscation, as long as KYC ((know your customer) and AML (anti money laundering) and other regulations are observed. It is understood that regulations regarding these nascent blockchain technologies, differ from jurisdiction to jurisdiction. In time various governments will introduce more regulations to ensure customer protection and generate revenue through taxes, etc. This, from the author's views will encourage wider use ushering crypto currencies into the mainstream.

Currently around 300 million people worldwide from the total global population of about 7.2b (a mere 3% of the total) are utilizing blockchain technologies and by extension crypto currencies.

As more governments launch regulations and acceptance of crypto currencies is embraced, we may in time expect a billion or more people utilizing crypto currencies.

"Be and become a disrupter and not disrupted"
-Pishu T.S

WORKING OF CRYPTO CURRENCIES

Crypto currencies are essentially enabled by blockchain technology. A blockchain is a digital publicly distributed ledger made up of increasing blocks of data. With a blockchain distributed public ledger, records of transactions can be kept across multiple computers on a network. Each computer is addressed as a node and, these nodes verify and store data precisely, accurately forever.

As new transactions are added to a block of data, then that particular block is added to the chain. The entire ledger is updated constantly and consistently as new transactions flow in. Almost all crypto experts say blockchain technologies have the tremendous potential to usher in the next evolution of the internet, presently designated as web3. Possibilities of web3 are massive going forward in time.

It is possible to utilize blockchain technologies across many traditional industries as well as nascent industries, not least personal finance, banking, investment, insurance, real estate, resource management, supply chain management, travel, logistics, shipping, gaming, metaverse, cross border payments, remote workers' payments, and various others not yet on the radar screens for most of us.

In order to complete transactions, one needs to pay the respective fees in the related crypto currencies. The fees vary from transaction to transaction, mostly depending on the time that the particular blockchain takes to complete. One needs to be very alert to fees charged and have the option to accept or reject.

> "Adapt an attitude to see and question 'what is this?'
> Do not assume. Learn moment to moment through
> lifelong learning and self-teaching"
> -Pishu T. S.

WHAT ARE THE WAYS TO KNOW CRYPTO CURRENCIES VALUES

The value of each crypto currency depends on several metrics. Presently with so many crypto currencies it can be very, very difficult to figure out which are actually and truly valuable. Like most other assets, demand and supply is one of the important issues in determining a given crypto currency's valuation. The more people use a coin or a blockchain of a coin, it is more likely to see an increase in demand and thereby price.

Very well-established crypto currencies viz. Bitcoin, Ethereum are used by more investors, institutes, small, medium, and large money managers, and the general public in addition to university endowments, investment banks, public listed corporations and even governments and therefore they have a higher value.

As more people use Bitcoin and Ethereum networks, the prices of Bitcoin and Ethereum as well as several popular ones, will tend to be higher than other crypto currencies.

Several experts also point to the 1st mover advantage enjoyed by Bitcoin, Ethereum and currently other 20 top listed or even 50 top listed crypto currencies.

Supply can also influence the price of a crypto currency, as well as investors understanding or expectation of its value.

Experts say Bitcoin is more likely to maintain its value as there is limited supply. Bitcoin systems deployed by its creators is fixed at 21m. This scarcity contributes to its value.

When selecting which crypto currency or currencies to invest in, it could be worthwhile to select coins that have a very strong use case, and high demand thereby greater chances of its greater adoption.

Ethereum is in a class of its own and is considered valuable after Bitcoin. This is mainly due to having capabilities of smart contracts. The ability to provide smart contracts makes it possible to build various applications not only for finance but several others including NFTs, etc.

"To replace doubts with certainty, do not just believe
Check evidence mathematically and scientifically"
-Pishu T. S.

HOW TO POSSIBLY BENEFIT FROM CRYPTO CURRENCIES?

Based on popularity of Bitcoin, Ethereum and smart contracts there are several ways to benefit from crypto currencies

1. Trading
2. Investing
3. Locked or normal Staking
4. Liquidity pool financing
5. Lending and earning
6. Farming

"Trials, retrials, failures
Are rungs of the ladder to success"
-Pishu T. S

HOW TO INVEST IN CRYPTO CURRENCIES?

One of the best ways is to set up an account with a centralized crypto currencies exchange. There are many different exchanges to choose from, based on the country you are in. Each exchange's rules and regulations are based on the jurisdiction they operate from.

Most popular crypto currencies exchanges are:

1. Binance
2. Coinbase
3. Kraken
4. Huobi
5. Toro
6. Swiss Borg
7. FTT

It is best to check each exchanges account opening procedures. In fact, it is advisable to get an account opened. Perform a dry run or test as to the exchanges account functions viz. depositing, withdrawing, buying, selling, trading fees, etc.

Only when satisfied with all features, then and only then activate the account to ensure easy and smooth operation. Some very busy exchanges may take a month or several months to set up an account.

"Create through knowledge
Innovate through confidence
Succeed through auspiciousness
Love through purity"

-Pishu T.S

HOW TO BUY CRYPTO CURRENCIES?

To buy crypto currencies one needs to choose a crypto currency exchange. Check the exchange's specific rules and conditions for opening an account. You will need to create an account with your real name, address, photo, contact details, etc. The exchange will verify the account and may ask you for other compliance requirements.

Once the account is opened, you will be directed for depositing funds, ordering the crypto currency or currencies of your choice, quantity required, etc.

A minimum amount may apply for an order which normally is quite low. Some start from as low as few hundred USD at Binance. Other exchanges should be checked out for the minimum amount permissible. The purchased crypto can be maintained at the exchange or transferred to one's personal wallet.

Wallets can be cold or hot. Cold wallets are individually owned and operated, whereas hot wallets are those of exchanges. If the purpose is trading, then the purchased cryptos can be retained at the exchange. The convenience of exchanges is that upon sale, the funds are credited immediately, normally within a few moments and can be reinvested in other choice crypto currencies. Upon purchase of any crypto currency or currencies, the funds are debited immediately.

"The potency of a seed is invisible"
-Pishu T.S

CONVERSION OF CRYPTO TO CASH

Again, the use of a centralized crypto currency exchange i.e. Binance is beneficial. One of the ways is to sell the crypto is through the exchange. There are several other ways as listed below:

- Peer to peer through the exchange

- Sell from your wallet

- Crypto debit cards

- Crypto currencies ATMs

"Patience, persistence, prudence, perseverance
Ensure achievement"

-Pishu T.S

IS THERE A MINIMUM AMOUNT REQUIRED FOR INVESTMENT IN CRYPTO CURRENCIES

In realty there are no minimums required to invest in any crypto currencies. Most exchanges allow purchase of nominal quantities. Others may have higher amount requirements. Many crypto currencies trade for less than a dollar in the present bear market trend prevalent since last five to seven months.

Crypto currencies can be very lucrative investments with very, very high returns in short periods of time or at the same time they can trend downwards based on news flows, policy changes, etc. Crypto currencies are extensively volatile and can go up or down anywhere by 15-20% and even up to 65-75% within a short period of time.

The author is strongly of the opinion that minute self-initiated extensive and detailed research, including one's own risk parameters, time horizons, returns expectation and liquidity, etc. needs to be conducted. Through this, one gains insights, knowledge, and understanding followed by action and pre-emption prior to committing a single dollar.

Know that markets and assets move independently of one's entry levels and ROI (return on investment) expectations. All asset classes are generally subject to news flow, be it specific, regional, national, or global as well as policy changes, regulations, etc.

At all times understand that the only certainty is uncertainty, and anything can happen at any time anywhere.

WHAT ARE STABLE COINS?

Stable coins are crypto currencies for which the price is pegged to another asset. These assets can be USD, Euro, commercial money markets paper, gold, or other crypto currency.

Popular stable coins are:

1. Tether (USDT)
2. Binance USD (BUSD)
3. Pax Dollar (USDP)
4. True USD (TUSD)
5. USD coin (USDC)
6. Dai (DAI)
7. Digix Gold Token (DGX)

WHAT ARE NFTS?

NFTs are digital products and can be created, bought, sold, held, gifted, or transferred. They exist on crypto currency wallets and are mostly stored in IPFs files (inter planetary file systems)

NFTs or non-fungible tokens are a unique token that is enabled through blockchain. Each NFT is authenticated, date and time stamped, and exists forever.

NFTs can be created of art, music, song, a real estate deed, an insurance policy, a contract, a commercial product, a branded product, or anything under the sun! An NFT can take the form of an image, a video, audio or mp4 track and more (limitations apply).

One can purchase an NFT because of its artistic nature or really any characteristic that appeals to you. NFTs have the ability to provide value to their creators and holders in a variety of ways:

1. Proof of authenticity.

2. Infinite life span (blockchain lives forever).

3. Crypto currency markets do not close and are open 24/7, 365 days.

4. Access to events, give aways, and discounts completely changes the game.

5. Holder rights +++.

6. Can continuously innovate and create.

7. Not every NFT needs to capitalize on the underlying tack.

8. Being an artist, minting a digital piece as art can go a long way, even without adding anything to the basics.

We live in a world that allows us to be unique in nearly anything we do and NFTs are unique. The beauty is one can create a single NFT that means 1/1 or multiple copies of each NFT (1 to 1k, 10k, 20k) known as sub-NFTs. It is understood that a unique 1/1 NFT can command a higher price than the one created in multiple copies of the same.

Like the blockchains and crypto currencies, NFTs can be utilized for various purposes. Amongst the traditional industries presently known, global brands utilizing NFTs for marketing their products are: Nike, Adidas, Prada, Christian Dior and several others, unknown to author. Market research can reveal details.

The author has from 2021 created over 3k NFTs of different themes. For the benefit of readers of this e-book, images of the NFTs with their captions are being posted separately.

List of popular technologies presently in use:

- Blockchains various
- AI - artificial intelligence
- VR - virtual realty
- AR - Augmented realty
- Hashgraph
- IOTA - internet of things

List of 20 top crypto currencies symbols names and current coins in issue

Bitcoin	21m
Ethereum	122.7m (coins in circulation to date)
USDT tether	6.01b
USDC	52,01b
BNB Binance coin	200 m
BUSD Binance stable coin	9.42b
Ada Cardano	45b
XRP ripple	9.99b
Sol soluna	523.90b
Doge	132b+++
Dot polka dot	1b
Matic polygon	10b
Dai dao (decentralized autonomous organization)	7.01b
Shib shiba inu	49.063b
Trx tron	99.28b
Avax avalanche	720m
Leo linus sed lee	985.24b
Wbtc wrapped Bitcoin	247,760
Uni uniswap	1b
Mtm magic internet money	457b

Essential websites:

www.cointelegraph.com for daily news

www.coincodex.com for each coins' current price market value etc

www.NFTcalendar.com for NFT promotions

www.NFTculture.com for NFT happenings and promotion

If you have reached to this part of the e-book, your devoted time and patience is commendable as it is obvious that you have a keen interest in blockchain technologies and crypto currencies. My good wishes follow you into your journey. Welcome to the world of Blockchain Technology!

With my sincere gratitude …

Without His Grace, not a single word in this e-book would have been scripted. With the glorious, gracious, precious, all-pervasive Divine Lord Kryshna's blessings and inner guidance, this e-book is now in your hands.

My immense gratitude to my precious wife, my 'doll' Naina, whose experience as a trained teacher has equipped her with an eye for detail especially in writing. Her proofreading abilities surpass, and I am grateful to her for devoting her valuable time to proofread and edit this e-book.

The Designer and the Doctor played an immense role in this e-book albeit remotely. My heartfelt gratitude to my beloved daughter, Natasha (The Designer) and her husband, Alok Madan (The Doctor). Natasha has been a friend, my constant support, my best critic, and my advisor for the longest time ever. Together I am grateful for their continuous encouragement and support. Their genuine awe of my self-acquired knowledge (thru lifelong learning and self-teaching) and self-developed skills have inspired further creative endeavours. Their belief in my efforts has resulted in a will to overcome all adversities, and boldly negotiate all turns and twists of life while attempting new and diverse projects through dreaming big and out of box thinking.

I would never dream of completing this acknowledgement without mention of my two beautiful and talented granddaughters Zindagi (11) and Zaia (8) for their creative contributions of eight images of artworks which I have added to my collection of NFTS! They do me proud.

Finally, my thanks and sincere appreciation to my senior publishing consultant, Ms. Jade Bailey for guiding me each step of the way before, during and after publication. My thanks also to my CIC (check in coordinator), PSA (publishing service associate) Ms. Kathy Lorenzo who has undertaken to run me through each aspect of publishing, this being my first ever e-book.

ABOUT THE AUTHOR

Life is dynamic and throws turns, twists and with this, opportunities unfold.

The Grace Divine has blessed each one of us with free will and the powers to gain knowledge, understanding and wisdom as well as strength to seek answers from within. Doing the right thing without deliberation or delay requires utilizing the five dynamic senses of hearing, seeing, smelling, tasting, and touching. Other senses that aid include our sense of intuition, our sense of imagination and vision. Exercising discipline and discrimination, and sometimes restraint and finally the sense of letting go or holding on are all conducive to growth.

Being a student of The Geeta and a Scorpio, my zodiac sign, I have been blessed with opportune occasions to let go or hold on - be it possessions, money, profit or loss, happiness or sadness, memories, relationships, or others in each of the seven dimensions of life.

My journey began almost six years ago. In 2016, I suffered a loss of over $3.5m! A local Hong Kong company supplied fake perfumes that resulted in my having to settle with cash refunds and free shipments to my overseas customers. Setbacks continued in 2017 with several customers delaying or not paying for delayed deliveries of Casio and Seiko watches affecting even my passionate Italian wine business!

Searching within for some income streams, I dabbled in Crypto currencies with baby steps, investing in a coin whose name and low price appealed to me. The coin's name is Ripple.

With health issues continuing from an earlier stroke, I decided to take off for a trip to USA to surprise our daughter for her 40th birthday. I flew out from Hong Kong on 28 October 2017 to be in Houston before 30 October, her birthday. Like me and my elder brother Hiro, my wife and daughter are also Scorpios. Each of us are characterized with different nature traits, despite being of the same birth sign!

On the flight the Lord threw an opportunity in my lap via an article on Satoshi Nakamoto's 9th anniversary of his White Paper on Bitcoin. With so much flight time on hand, I read the entire article. It intrigued me and seemed challenging. Then and there, I started formulating a strategy to know, learn, adapt, and devote time and some money to Bitcoin.

Fortunately I was able to gain access to a 10-course lesson from Mr. Roger Ver, CEO of bitcoin.com. Since then, I have since developed a profound respect for the BTC evangelist. First, I entered a mining contract with bitcoin.com. Subsequently, I purchased 0.14 BTC and then when markets came down, I further purchased 0.16 BTC. Since then, I have sold at around USD64k x 1BTC grossing ten times the amount invested!

Prior to this in March 2017, I had read about Crypto currencies and selected a single coin whose name and low price appealed to me. I invested €700.61. Being a nomad and not knowing much about wallets, etc. I surrendered to the European broker and got back €670. I took a loss of €30.61, writing that off as my cost of learning. Since then I have taken a keen and holistic long-term approach to Crypto currencies, NFTs, staking, etc.

In 2018 with my growing interest in Blockchain technology and Crypto currencies, I started to write a blog post entitled DigitalInsights18.com. I also signed up on Quora and before I knew it, I was answering various critical questions on blockchain technology and crypto currencies. In the last six months, have had over 120,000 views, and over 150 upvotes in addition to over 100 comments! Many of these comments and queries are from regular investors, accomplished bankers and the like. Being a people person and always wanting to share my knowledge has been the inspiration to pen this e-book.

Cryptocurrency markets over time have corelated with traditional markets and continue to be not only volatile but also in tandem on macro levels with money market funds, interest rates as well as tech stocks. They have been down since the last seven months.

Being a student of The Geeta, Blockchain, Crypto currencies as well as Fibonacci sequences, I am confident the wondrous, irreversible, industrial, immutable blockchain technologies will continue to be vastly adapted. Crypto currencies, NFTs, etc. are enabled and sustained by blockchain technologies and will continue to march forward in mainstream adaption by almost all traditional industries and nascent industries, many of which are not even on the radar screens for most of us!

Ripple (payment protocol)

From Wikipedia, the free encyclopedia

Ripple is a real-time gross settlement system (RTGS), currency exchange and remittance network by Ripple. Also called the **Ripple Transaction Protocol** (RTXP) or **Ripple protocol**,[3] it is built upon a distributed open source Internet protocol, consensus ledger and native currency called XRP (ripples). Released in 2012, Ripple purports to enable "secure, instant and nearly free global financial transactions of any size with no chargebacks." It supports tokens representing fiat currency, cryptocurrency, commodity or any other unit of value such as frequent flier miles or mobile minutes.[4][5] At its core, Ripple is based around a shared, public database or ledger,[6] which uses a consensus process that allows for payments, exchanges and remittance...[7]

Ripple	
Original author(s)	Arthur Britto, David Schwartz, Ryan Fugger
Developer(s)	Ripple
Initial release	2012
Stable release	0.60.0 / 2017[8]
Repository	github.com/ripple/rippled (https://github.com/ripple/rippled)
Development status	Active

Contents

Bitcoin Address Addresses are identifiers which you use to send bitcoins to another person.

Summary

Address	1JdLSZfDnvvhVPsoDdRVffC3GfUSGW5Mmf
Hash 160	c159575d0bc59907d62dbf0e002bd42703c9ccb7

Transactions

No. Transactions	2
Total Received	0.3 BTC
Final Balance	0.3 BTC

Request Payment   Donation Button

Transactions (Oldest First)

Filter⌄

Bitcoin has been the best performing currency 3 of the last 4 years.
BUY YOURS NOW

BLOCKCHAIN

feaf1bfa4c0fc0c127797f8f547f0307eab29aa6a1ee3528a8df7a72d770e64e   **2018-08-10 10:09:52**

36pQjvNMRiufycBCbyGsFZDRey48Xpqcgu
3QokXhzCzmgBXE8uo15NBYG1Yc6j1s66kP
3LNQ8gVpLtiCWZXmu3Bd8S6BTvCeJBfMx1
3Ddfi95G6pxkrzhCCv7aBHvu1L9RMMkD43
33gJP8wrzUrzWfBnYv8jub7k59ZR34fMa7
3MfdMojUD1MPFmndMu4gYfvFg921ou7GQ6   ➡ 1JdLSZfDnvvhVPsoDdRVffC3GfUSGW5Mmf 0.16 BTC

18

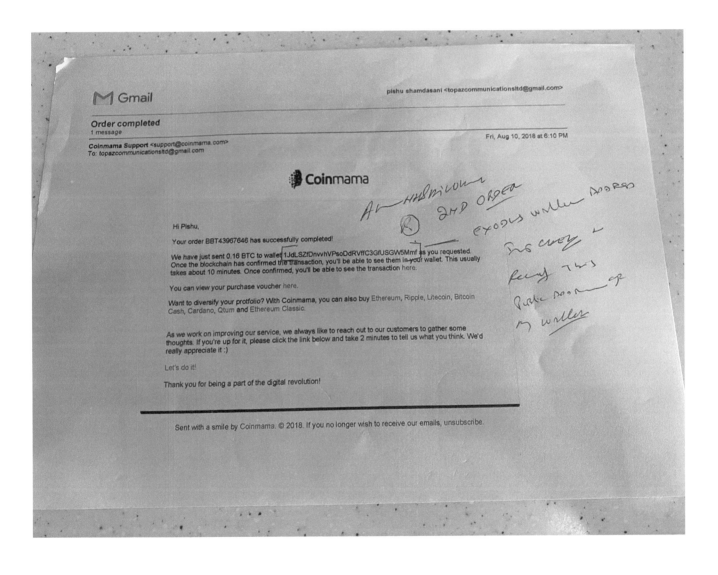

English ▾ | Sign out (/en/logout)

₿ BTC ↥ €1,064.590000 (/en/buy/bitcoin)	Ⓛ LTC ↥ €7.894460 (/en/buy/litecoin)	▲ ARDR ↥ €0.022104 (/en/buy/ardor)	ⓩ ZEC ↥ €59.753100 (/en/buy/zcash)
Ⓝ NAV ↥ €0.094157 (/en/buy/navcoin)	Ⓐ ABY ↥ €0.000278 (/en/buy/artbyte)	STRAT ↥ €0.289267 (/en/buy/stratis)	CCRB ↥ €0.827077 (/en/buy/cryptocarb
⬡ SDC ↥	RADS ↥	XEM ↥	♦ ETH ↥

⌄

Verification for tier 2 has been submitted

✅ Account activated   ✅ Tier 1   Tier 2 ▶ Tier 3   Fully verified

Tier 2 Verification

We are reviewing your verification request. In most cases we will process your verification within 1 business day.

Address

41n block 2, royal peninsula, hung hom bay,

Zipcode

852-22434010   *22424010*

City

kowloon, hongkong.

Document

Browse...

20

From: Coinmama Support
Sent: Wednesday, 10 January 2018 6:52 PM
To: topazcommunicationsltd@gmail.com
Subject: Order completed

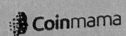

Hi Pishu,

Your order BBT32623440 has successfully completed!

We have just sent 0.14 BTC to wallet 1JdLSZfDnvvhVPsoDdRVffC3GfUSGW5Mmf. Once the Blockchain has confirmed the transaction, you'll be able to see them here or by going to your wallet. This may take up to 10 minutes.

You can view your purchase voucher here.

As we work on improving our service, we always like to reach out to our customers to gather some thoughts. If you're up for it, please click the link below and take 3 minutes to tell us what you think. We'd really appreciate it :)

Let's do it!

Thank you for being a part of the digital revolution.

Sent with a smile by Coinmama. © 2017. If you no longer wish to receive our emails, unsubscribe.

21

pishu shamdasani <topazcommunicationsltd@gmail.com>

Re: Fwd: Signed invoice
1 message

Fri, Jan 12, 2018 at 12:11 PM

Natalia Ra <natalia@bitcoin.com>
To: pishu shamdasani <topazcommunicationsltd@gmail.com>

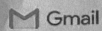 12/1/18

Dear Pishu,

Thank you so much for your patience. The bank finally confirmed the funds and your account is now active.

Please provide detail of the fees that were taken out from the returned funds (Just a snapshot of the statement amount) and we will credit that to your account as well.

Thank you and we sincerely appreciate your business.

Best regards,
Natalia

On 1/10/18 9:47 PM, pishu shamdasani wrote:

> Aum....
> Dear Natalia Ra,
> Trust all is well.
> Surprised we have not heard from you since 27th December.
>
> As requested by you we have sent you the invoice duly signed.
>
> Please confirm that the amount is already credit to your company by your bank and also please inform us about the status of our account as well as the bitcoin contract.
>
> Awaiting your early response.
> Wish you a happy fortune filled 2018.
>
> Warm regards.
>
> On 27 Dec 2017 13:33, "pishu shamdasani" <topazcommunicationsltd@gmail.com> wrote:
>
>> Aum....
>> Dear Natalia Ra,
>> Please find attached signed invoice as requested by you.
>>
>> Trust this will now enable you to get the funds in your company's account.
>>
>> Do please acknowledge receipt n let me know when our account will be activated.
>>
>> Thanks.Warm regards.

🎲 User Profile

A. Hoↄ̫ↄↄↄↄↄↄↄↄ 5-2-18

zznnpal1
0.011 780 32 BTC (withdraw)

👤 User Account - zznnpal1

Workers	1 Active, 0 Offline (workers)
Joined Date	2017-12-07
Total Earned	0.011 780 32 BTC
Payout Reward Type	PPS (Paid every 6:00AM UTC)

[Handwritten annotations at top of page:]

CARRY on FR STRATEGIES
28-10-17 on Flight LHC-USA
A — NEW DISCLOSURE
Pref, Minute Self identifies, Knowledge, Understanding,
Instincts, Decision, Self, Preemption.

[Handwritten annotations in left margin:]

U.U.U Send go-s
formula:
Story
re looked 4 non-owner
The peer - focus on
① BTC, ② IOTA ③ ETH
④ arm 5 arm 6 arm
7 arm 8 arm
Bear = 8 CORNERS
8 active
Any 1 on 2 corners
Can Be Damaged
But Root Will
Evolve

Bitcoin: A Peer-to-Peer Electronic Cash System

Satoshi Nakamoto
satoshin@gmx.com
www.bitcoin.org

Abstract. A purely peer-to-peer version of electronic cash would allow online payments to be sent directly from one party to another without going through a financial institution. Digital signatures provide part of the solution, but the main benefits are lost if a trusted third party is still required to prevent double-spending. We propose a solution to the double-spending problem using a peer-to-peer network. The network timestamps transactions by hashing them into an ongoing chain of hash-based proof-of-work, forming a record that cannot be changed without redoing the proof-of-work. The longest chain not only serves as proof of the sequence of events witnessed, but proof that it came from the largest pool of CPU power. As long as a majority of CPU power is controlled by nodes that are not cooperating to attack the network, they'll generate the longest chain and outpace attackers. The network itself requires minimal structure. Messages are broadcast on a best effort basis, and nodes can leave and rejoin the network at will, accepting the longest proof-of-work chain as proof of what happened while they were gone.

1. Introduction

Commerce on the Internet has come to rely almost exclusively on financial institutions serving as trusted third parties to process electronic payments. While the system works well enough for most transactions, it still suffers from the inherent weaknesses of the trust based model. Completely non-reversible transactions are not really possible, since financial institutions cannot avoid mediating disputes. The cost of mediation increases transaction costs, limiting the minimum practical transaction size and cutting off the possibility for small casual transactions, and there is a broader cost in the loss of ability to make non-reversible payments for non-reversible services. With the possibility of reversal, the need for trust spreads. Merchants must be wary of their customers, hassling them for more information than they would otherwise need. A certain percentage of fraud is accepted as unavoidable. These costs and payment uncertainties can be avoided in person by using physical currency, but no mechanism exists to make payments over a communications channel without a trusted party.

What is needed is an electronic payment system based on cryptographic proof instead of trust, allowing any two willing parties to transact directly with each other without the need for a trusted third party. Transactions that are computationally impractical to reverse would protect sellers from fraud, and routine escrow mechanisms could easily be implemented to protect buyers. In this paper, we propose a solution to the double-spending problem using a peer-to-peer distributed timestamp server to generate computational proof of the chronological order of transactions. The system is secure as long as honest nodes collectively control more CPU power than any cooperating group of attacker nodes.

1

(https://www.bitcoin.com/)

BTC/USD	BCH/USD	menu
BTC/USD $17284	$1709	

(https://pr/bit.bitchir/mahit.coin.com/)

Oct 31, 2017 | Jamie Redman (https://news.bitcoin.com/author/jamieredman) | bitcoin.com

Satoshi Nakamoto's Brilliant White Paper Turns 9-Years Old

(https://news.bitcoin.com/wp-content/uploads/2017/10/Satoshi-Nakamotos-Brilliant-White-Paper-Turns-9-Years-Old-1.jpg)

AUM....

(1) READ, Analyze, Good insights, knowledge, understanding, action + preconception.

(2) Can bitcoin.com itself - all team members

(3) Change others related articles by comm members - can + see changes — seek opportunity deeper

(4) Disclosure → come offers of B/C — offer in bloc stars base

25

(handwritten) AL M228 ...

English ▼ | Sign out (/en/logout)

₿ BTC ⤴ €1,155.580000 (/en/buy/bitcoin)	**Ⓛ LTC ⤴** €11.599700 (/en/buy/litecoin)	**▲ ARDR ⤴** €0.023006 (/en/buy/ardor)	**ⓩ ZEC ⤴** €57.200000 (/en/buy/zcash)
N NAV ⤴ €0.084550 (/en/buy/navcoin)	**Ⓐ ABY ⤴** €0.000289 (/en/buy/artbyte)	**◇ STRAT ⤴** €0.504171 (/en/buy/stratis)	**Ⓒ CCRB ⤴** €0.726654 (/en/buy/cryptocarb
◈ SDC ⤴	**Ⓡ RADS ⤴**	**Ⓧ XEM ⤴**	**♦ ETH ⤴**

Complete your transaction

(handwritten) Imp: Series TT Tomorow
TT Send on 7-3-17
Htd 1,674

To complete your transaction wire €200.61 to our bank account. Include the unique identifier shown below in your transaction, this way we can match your transaction to your purchase.

(handwritten) Order 2 on
28-4-17

LBSC2260 You must include this in your transaction

(handwritten) LB100858
1300 euro 61:

Order details

Order Date	06-04-2017 13:03
Order Amount	200.00*
Order Total	**€200.61**

Litebit bank

Account holder	2525 Ventures BV
IBAN	NL22ABNA0544878264
BIC/swift	ABNANL2A

26

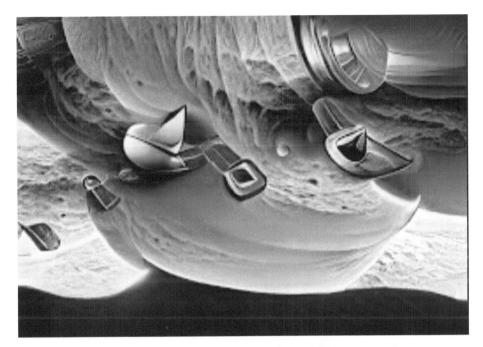

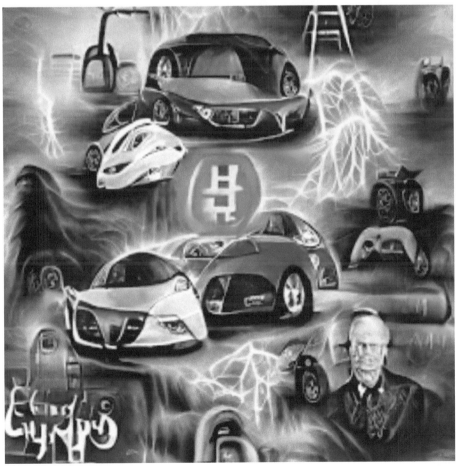

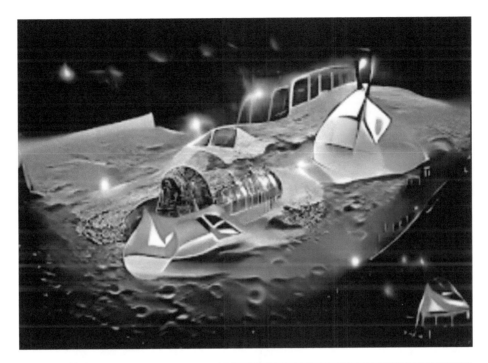

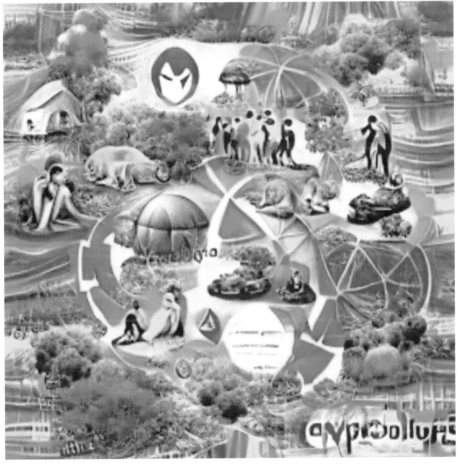

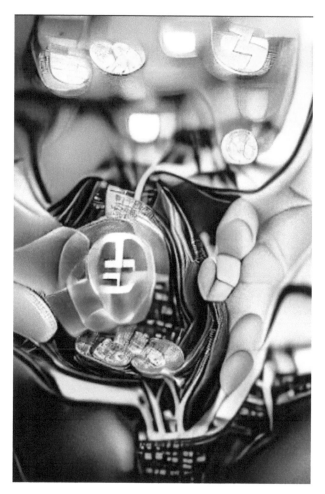

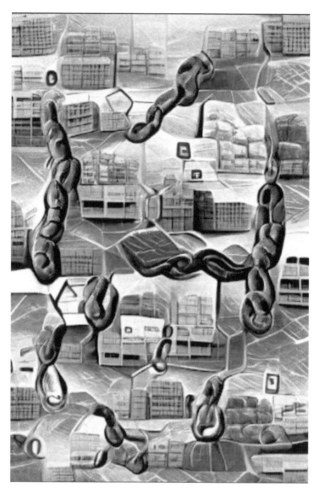

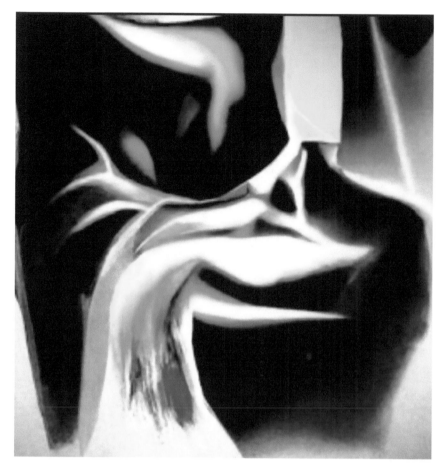

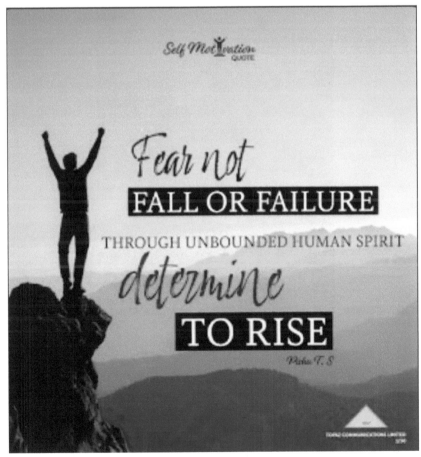

EACH ONE OF US IS A SOUL WITH A
BODY.
LET US TOGATHER SHARE
CONSCIOUSLY
LOVE PURE KIND
GRATITUDE
LIGHT
CARE
AND DO OUR BIT FOR GOOD AND
GREATER GOOD
A ACT OF SERENDIPTY

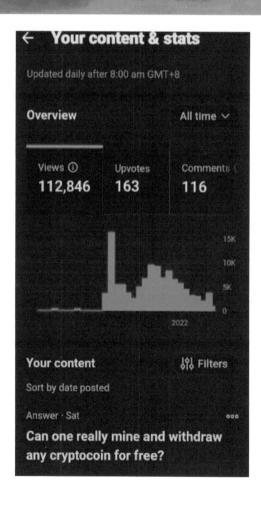

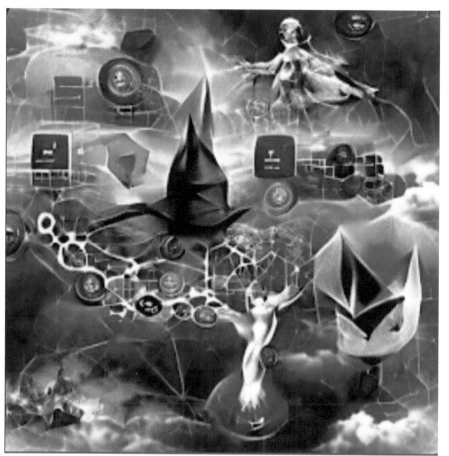

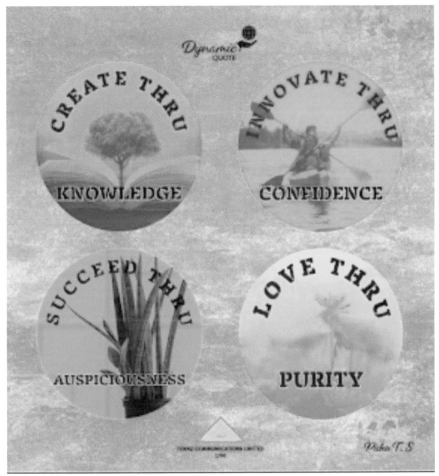